HARNESSING THE POWER AT YOUR FINGERTIPS

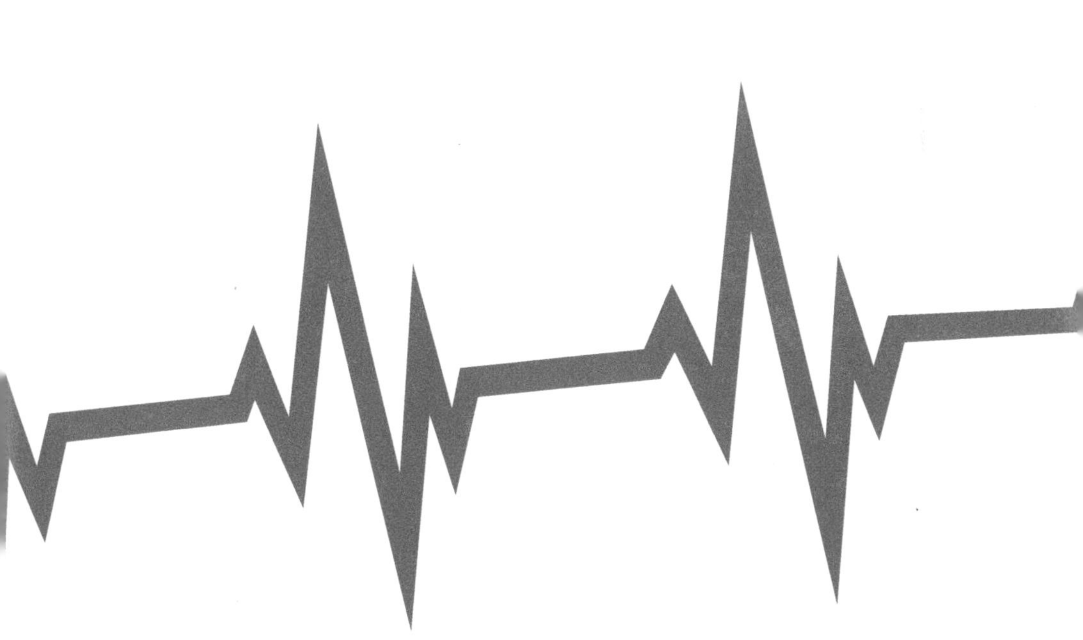

First published in 2020 by
CUTTING THROUGH THE BULL PUBLISHING

ISBN 978-1-8383488-0-9

Also available as an ebook
ISBN 978-1-8383488-1-6

dominicwalters.net

CUTTING THROUGH THE BULL
PUBLISHING

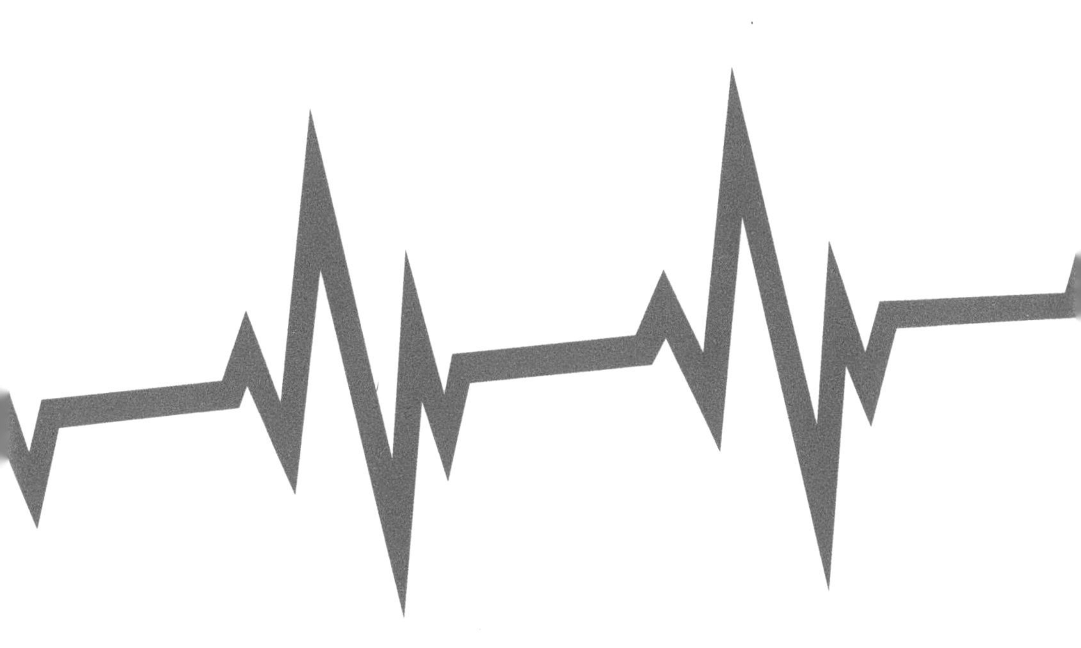

HARNESSING THE POWER AT YOUR FINGERTIPS

A LEADER'S GUIDE TO B2B MARKETING COMMUNICATIONS

DOMINIC WALTERS

HARNESSING THE POWER AT YOUR FINGERTIPS

B2B LEADERS

YOUR QUICK GUIDE TO THE POWER OF MARKETING COMMUNICATIONS AND WHY IT IS SO IMPORTANT TO YOUR STRATEGY AND BUSINESS

CUTTING THROUGH THE BULL – THE SERIES

A LEADER'S GUIDE TO B2B MARKETING COMMUNICATIONS

About the series

Each part of this short series is developed to be a quick read – with simple insights – to help you grasp the fundamental power of marketing communications. It is designed to enable you to start getting the most out of marketing communications in your business whilst avoiding all the bull.

Read this and let your marketing professionals take care of the rest. This is for you!

CONTENTS

INTRODUCTION 10

CHAPTER 1
WHAT IS THIS ALL ABOUT? 12

CHAPTER 2
5 SIMPLE TRUTHS 18

CHAPTER 3
4 COMMON MISTAKES 52

CHAPTER 4
3 MYTHS 64

CHAPTER 5
2 TIPS 72

CHAPTER 6
1 CONCLUSION 74

SO... WHERE DOES THAT LEAVE US? 76

CLOSING THOUGHTS 80

ACKNOWLEDGEMENTS 82

ABOUT THE AUTHOR 83

INTRODUCTION

HARNESSING THE POWER AT YOUR FINGERTIPS

"We sell to other businesses, not consumers"

"Our products are so good they will sell themselves"

Over the years, I have often heard these phrases uttered in the corridors of B2B businesses which is part of the reason I put together this short series. *Harnessing The Power At Your Fingertips*, the first instalment, is the natural starting point.

Marketing communications really is the secret weapon that every business leader should have at their fingertips and know how to unleash to protect their business and support their short-, mid- and long-term strategies.

CHAPTER ONE

WHAT IS THIS ALL ABOUT?

In 25 years of working for organisations of all shapes and sizes around the world, I have seen first hand how powerful a well-considered integrated marketing communications strategy can be, and the dramatic impact it has on a business's objectives, sales, growth plans and reputation.

I've also seen how the world of marketing communications is often misunderstood and certainly not leveraged in a way that fully unleashes its potential as a key pillar in driving and supporting business strategy.

While many people will spend their career focused on one or two specific disciplines, I have been fortunate enough to follow a rather unconventional career path. I have had roles and jobs that have enabled me to manage and leverage multiple disciplines at the same time to drive a business's agenda forward and build, protect and defend its reputation.

Solving challenges or problems across a range of sectors and in different regions of the world, I have dived deeply into the worlds of government, employee, investor and public relations right through to advertising, brand, reputation (launching, building and protecting) and the complex world of digital and social ecosystems.

As a result, I've been able to see how powerful the amazing disciplines that make up marketing communications can be when used correctly. Just as importantly, I have also seen how much time and money can be wasted when they are used incorrectly.

I'm passionate about the power of marketing communications and I believe that it should be a core pillar in any organisation – dramatically impacting how you drive, manage and protect growth, reputation and even the value of your business. I hope when you finish this book you will look at the world of marketing communications differently and recognise why it is so important.

MARKETING COMMUNICATIONS, INTEGRATED MARKETING COMMUNICATIONS?

You'll see a few phrases cropping up time and again throughout the book – marketing communications, integrated marketing communications, brand, narrative – so I want to be clear on what I mean.

MARKETING COMMUNICATIONS

I always refer to myself as a marketing communications professional – not just communications and not solely marketing.

Good marketing communications can be made up of one or more of the following disciplines and skills: public, government and employee relations; digital and brand management; social media; SEO; design; creative; advertising; writing; video production and storytelling.

This is not an exhaustive list, but it does convey the complexity and breadth of skills and knowledge that should be part of your marketing communications fire-power depending on which markets and sectors you operate within.

While some of these disciplines traditionally fall under communications and others would fall under marketing, their relationship is so intertwined I do not like to separate them.

I am not, of course, suggesting you employ all of these all the time – but it is unlikely that any organisation can deliver a good marketing communications strategy without combining many of these at any one time. Hence my use of both words together.

INTEGRATED MARKETING COMMUNICATIONS

The word "integrated" has been around for a long time in my profession. It has become an overused phrase that rarely lives up to what we should expect from true integrated marketing communications. I once asked a PR agency about the "integrated" strategy of which they were very proud. This turned out to be distributing a press release to all the target newspapers and media via email but also converting the press release into a pdf and uploading it onto the corporate website accompanied by a tweet – that was integrated!

To me – and this is something I will unpack in more detail in my next book *Shooting for the Stars* – integrated marketing communications refers to the ability to leverage each and every discipline, as appropriate, to deliver powerful outcomes that underpin a business's strategy. Done correctly, it is not only more impactful but can actually be much better value for the business, allowing budgets to be stretched further.

"Your brand is what people say about you when you are not in the room"

BRAND

If you were to search this term online, you would find many different definitions. It is not your logo, or your product name printed on a label – those are just visual components of the brand, visual representations of your company or product name. Today a strong brand represents your business's personality, vision, values – it helps to define who you are and what you stand for. It is the sum total of every touchpoint your customer has with your business. It should build trust in your business and drive credibility. It has a lot to do!

Your brand underpins so many parts of your business that it is effectively your DNA – a phrase you will find I use interchangeably with brand.

NARRATIVE

Narrative is another phrase you will come across liberally sprinkled throughout this book. Simply, your narrative is a component of your brand and one of the ways you express it. While your brand should be the foundation of your business's personality, your narrative can evolve and stretch as you share your corporate, product and value story. A narrative should always align with your brand, but the message and emphasis of your narrative can and should change and flex to suit your audience.

CHAPTER TWO

5 SIMPLE TRUTHS

Marketing communications is vital in building protecting and driving your business's reputation

Marketing communications is not sales, but it is strategically fundamental to sales

Marketing communications should underpin employee morale & drive an army of product & brand advocates

Marketing communications agencies make a significant difference – when leveraged correctly

Marketing communications can add **$$$** value to your business

Marketing communications is vital in building, protecting and driving your business's reputation

DEFINING, CLARIFYING AND SHARING YOUR VISION & VALUES

TELLING YOUR STORY

ESTABLISHING YOUR CREDIBILITY

BUILDING TRUST IN YOUR BUSINESS

BUILDING & PROTECTING YOUR REPUTATION

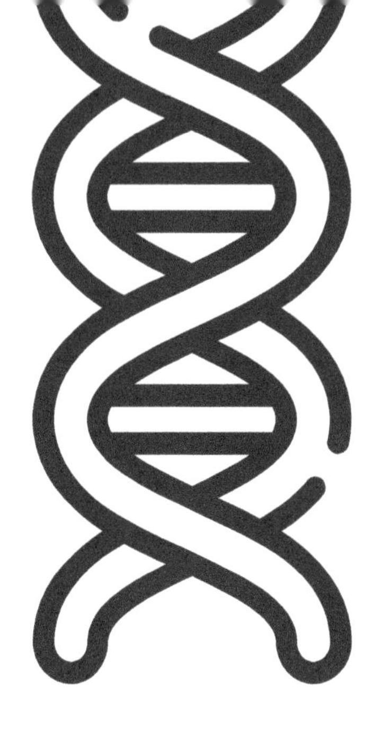

How a business is perceived by the stake-holders and businesses it engages with, or wants to engage with, will be critical to whether it succeeds or fails. No one will be a stranger to words like credibility, trust, reliability, experience, innovation, vision, consistency and so on. These words, or similar, will underpin your reputation and, depending on how you operate, will need to "live and breathe" across your business and the audiences you want to work with. Some may call the foundations for this your "narrative" or "story". I would say it is so much more – it is your DNA.

Your DNA is how you, your employees and your products are seen by the world and it is what underpins your reputation. That DNA can be your energy and force for growth.

Your story, message, narrative, image, values, and vision are all key components to demonstrating what your business does, how it does it, and what it stands for. Today, more than ever, your customers want to know who you are, if they can trust you, if you share their values, and if you will be there in the tough times as well as the good ones.

Building this story and embedding your DNA internally and externally takes time and effort. It should be reflected in your speeches, events, annual reports, brochures, sales language, advertising, messaging and digital channels, to name just a few.

It certainly does not happen overnight, but once in place it is an immensely powerful and important part of your business – some may even say it is the beating heart of your business, energising the workforce.

However, if we have learnt anything from the world today, protecting your reputation is as important as building it. Times of crisis, product issues and leadership scandals don't just disappear; in fact, "untreated", your reputation may never recover from a setback. More worrying is that it takes a considerable amount of time and effort to build your reputation but very little time to damage it.

It is the marketing communications professionals that will help you define and articulate your DNA before embedding it internally and externally and ensuring that it is set up to build, defend and protect the business. They are the guardians of your DNA – they will be responsible for keeping that heart energised and beating strongly.

SO WHAT?

You may well ask. Consider how hard it is to build your reputation, credibility and trust. Defining your brand – who you are and what you stand for – is the starting point and becomes your differentiator in a competitive world.

Living and breathing in our "always-on" news cycle means you have to work harder than ever to manage your brand, and it also means that your reputation is constantly at risk.

Consider significant activist criticism, or a competitor aggressively attacking your business, or a serious product failure. No business is immune to this type of crisis, but some are better prepared than others.

Your brand is bit like an insurance policy: investing in it during the good times is important. How you manage and nurture your brand will determine how audiences react when you have to respond to a crisis. Are your trust and credibility sufficiently strong to carry your customers and stakeholders as you weather a storm or two? It can be the difference between keeping your hard-won reputation and losing it. No one wants to spend months, years or even decades building trust and credibility in their underlying brand only to lose it overnight because they failed to react or handle a bad situation correctly.

"IT TAKES MANY GOOD DEEDS TO BUILD A REPUTATION, AND ONLY ONE BAD ONE TO LOSE IT"

BENJAMIN FRANKLIN

INTEL

CHIP MANUFACTURER, MICROPROCESSOR, THE BRAIN INSIDE YOUR COMPUTER?

In the 90s and early noughties, "Intel Inside" and its Pentium processor were phrases synonymous with the battle to sell computers. What makes this so interesting is the fact that Intel was a B2B business chip manufacturer supplying some of the world's most powerful computer brands. Intel's clever messaging became a central theme for its customers' advertising.

Its approach increased its relevance and importance in the supply chain from chip manufacturer to the "brain inside your computer" — something consumers expected and asked for when buying.

There is no question that Intel treated its brand more like a B2C one, but this is a great example of how a B2B business shaped its narrative, created a powerful story for all its audiences and ensured that its direct customers (not the consumer) fully embraced it.

What made this clever? It was simple, clear and easy for everyone in the supply chain to understand. A powerful and simple message from a supplier is compelling and cuts through the bull, especially if it remains relevant from the factory floor right through to the shop window.

ADOBE

PDF CREATOR, DESIGN TOOL, CREATIVE PLATFORM?

Adobe is a business that has touched nearly all of us in one way or another. The most obvious will be our friend the pdf!

Back in the early 90s, Adobe was at the forefront of desktop publishing, selling CDs with its publishing software on them that were used by a specific group of businesses. Today, Adobe is one of the most successful SaaS businesses in the world with annual revenues hitting $95 billion. Its core products have evolved and infrastructure has changed dramatically but its vision and focus has always remained consistent – the tool shop of the creative. Today Adobe uses phrases like “creativity is in our DNA” and “democratising creativity”.

As it has successfully transitioned from desktop publisher to a SaaS supplying creative tools from the cloud it has not lost sight of who its audience is and what its purpose has been. It is this narrative and focus that has remained simple and consistent, ensuring that its global reputation is clearly understood and its credibility remains firmly intact with a powerful DNA – the guardian of creativity.

Marketing communications is not sales, but it is strategically fundamental to sales

PROMOTING YOUR PRODUCTS?

LAUNCHING A NEW PRODUCT?

OPENING IN A NEW MARKET?

ENTERING A NEW SECTOR?

FILLING THE SALES FUNNEL?

TARGETING YOUR CUSTOMERS WITH RELEVANT MESSAGING?

TAKING ON THE COMPETITION?

How do new prospects, suppliers, customers, and potential advocates know who you are, what you offer and how you stack up against the competition and trust what you offer? How does your product get noticed, get differentiated, and break through the noise? A large part of this will be down to the marketing communications strategy that is shaped around your product and sales cycle. It will be down to the narrative, proof points, tools and credibility of the business and its products. Also, your reliability and track record of historic products or services and the way the industry reacts and talks about your business will play an important part in how people engage with you. In turn, much of this will then drive how you launch new products or enter new markets – do you disrupt with a bold and brash approach or will it be a graceful and elegant entrance?

ONE TEAM – ONE VICTORY, A SALE, CONTRACT, SIGNATURE, DEAL!

Celebrations, congratulations, press releases and parties often accompany the signing of a contract. Heroes of the moment are praised, rewarded and celebrated – deservedly so! However, in the heat of the moment and celebrations, it often surprises me how little credit goes to the efforts that got the product or service into the market, built its credibility, shaped the story that underpinned its benefits, brought it to life against the competition and even protected it throughout the tough times.

Though it's common sense, it is sometimes worth highlighting that sales rarely "just happens". Take Newton's Cradle – the last ball is not going to swing if the first one does not kick off the process, driving it to the next ball, then the next and so on. Similarly, sealing a deal requires several steps to reach that final sale or contract signature.

Marketing communications will kick off the momentum, building awareness then moving on to educating audiences before swinging on to establish credibility. After this the goal of marketing communications is to keep the buzz and energy going while the sales team takes the process through the funnel. So to help break this down, what could this look like if you were activating your business and products in a new market? Well, it is unlikely you will achieve the most impact just from getting your sales teams to start calling all potential prospects out of the blue. An integrated strategy clearly takes the company brand and product story through a series of phases, laying the foundations for sales to open a "friendly" door and start talking.

According to research by Accenture in 2018, most B2B buyers are 57% of the way through the buying process before the first meeting. That finding emphasises the importance of ensuring that the narrative around the business, products and services is rock solid, or there will not be a first meeting.

WORTH NOTING

NEW TO CREDIBLE

UNKNOWN TO KNOWN

UNPROVEN TO TRUSTED

TALK TO SALE

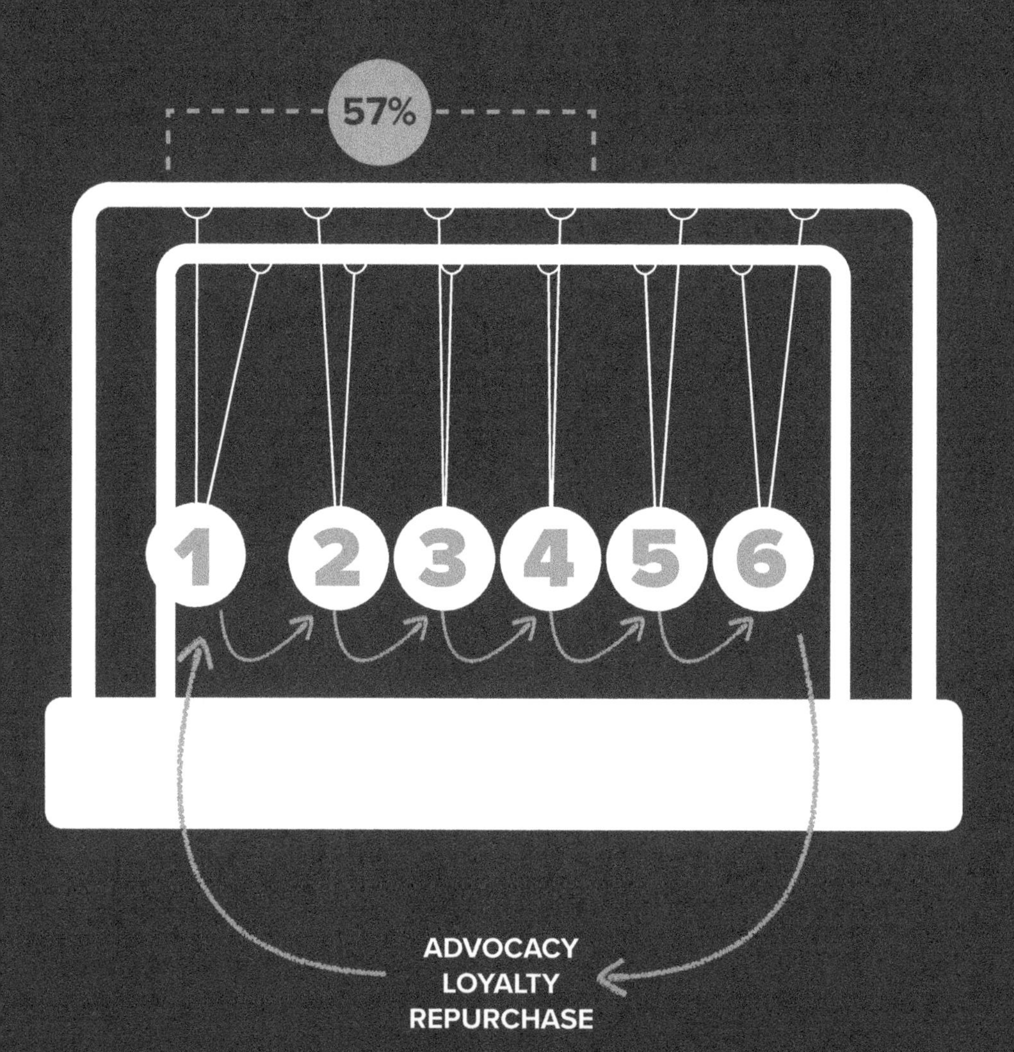

1. **CREATE AWARENESS** – LAUNCH IN THE MARKET (PR, MARKETING, EVENTS, BROCHURES)
2. **BUILD FAMILIARITY** – EDUCATE AND BUILD CUSTOMER KNOWLEDGE OF THE BENEFITS (BROCHURES, DEMONSTRATIONS, MEDIA, TRADE MEDIA)
3. **BE CONSIDERED** – BUILD CREDIBILITY AND SHOW WHY IT IS GREAT (THOUGHT LEADERSHIP, PR, PROMOTE SUCCESSES)
4. **ENGAGE & CONVINCE** THAT THE PRODUCT IS RIGHT (LISTEN, CUSTOMISE, PRICE, EXPLAIN, EVENTS, DEMOS)
5. **CONVERT & NEGOTIATE** AND PREPARE FOR A SALE (PR, LAUNCHES, EVENTS)
6. **DO THE DEAL** – SIGN THE CONTRACT

Many will recognise this as a straightforward B2B sales cycle, and it is. However, it is important to recognise how important marketing communications is throughout the process – not a nice-to-have, but critical.

Doing the deal is clearly only the beginning, and we touch on this in the next section.

PLAYING TO MULTIPLE AUDIENCES & THE LONG SALES CYCLE GAME

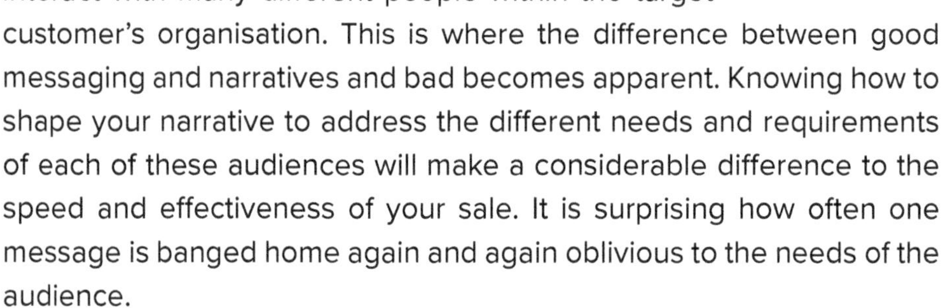

Another area important to recognise is the complexity of your customers' purchasing process and the long sales cycle – something that is not uncommon in the B2B world. A sales team may have to interact with many different people within the target customer's organisation. This is where the difference between good messaging and narratives and bad becomes apparent. Knowing how to shape your narrative to address the different needs and requirements of each of these audiences will make a considerable difference to the speed and effectiveness of your sale. It is surprising how often one message is banged home again and again oblivious to the needs of the audience.

The other side of this complex coin is long sales cycles. If a sale takes 12–24 months, your sales team cannot simply bang on the door of a prospect every 2–4 weeks offering to tell them about the product. Once is great – twice is fantastic – after that it is beginning to look like harassment. As your prospect meets your competition (which they are going to do), maintaining your company credibility and superior product story, whilst ensuring that your offer is not forgotten, is vital to staying in the game.

Maintaining your edge, relevance and credibility is crucial if your sales team is going to get to the finishing line. This is done by combining a wide range of marketing communications techniques to keep your business in play and make sure that when the time is right, you are a contender – and hopefully the winner.

SIGNING THE DEAL, MAKING THE SALE

Signing the deal is only the beginning of what will hopefully be a long-term relationship. Now you will need to maintain your credibility and the trust placed in you, whilst also ensuring that you constantly remind your customer that they made the right choice.

You will have account managers or relationship managers whose job will be to keep managing the customer after a sale. But who is maintaining your public reputation, ensuring the products and your brand are seen as the leaders in the field? As competitors put new products into the market, who is evolving your message to ensure that your story demonstrates you are still the best? Marketing Communications – their job never ends. It is a continuous cycle for the team, but they are now supporting different people with messaging.

Whilst teams around your business will be fulfilling the contract, it is highly likely that you are hoping to build that customer relationship, sell more in the future and ensure that you maintain the preferred supplier position. Obviously, fulfilling the contract on budget and time is important, but credibility and trust must be maintained and the reputation you want your customer to recognise you for has to be managed. PR, thought leadership, advertising, events and advocacy are all key to this.

Marketing communications should underpin employee morale & drive an army of product & brand advocates

YOUR GLOBAL AMBASSADORS

DEFINE
WHO YOU ARE

LIVE
YOUR VISION & VALUES

PROMOTE
YOUR PRODUCTS

CHAMPION
YOUR BUSINESS IN YOUR REGIONS & SECTORS

> **Your employees are three times more reliable than the CEO. Employee advocacy, engagement or its absence will inevitably affect the perception of your brand**
>
> **Edelman Trust Barometer 2016**

Our reputation, values and vision start at home! Employees are an asset that demonstrate and amplify your business values by understanding what you stand for, and they should live and breathe your story. They are a major portion of your DNA and beating heart.

They can be a passionate and powerful army of advocates singing your praises, building and amplifying a positive story, or they can be a thorn in your side when morale is low and trust in your leadership is fading.

Keeping them engaged, energised and enthusiastic is a full-time job. Marketing Communications and HR need to work closely together and should be aware that this is more than employee engagement – a mistake often made. To create an army of advocates means starting with knowing what your business stands for, where it is going and why – and then exciting and energising your employees by ensuring they believe in your brand. Essentially you need to embed your brand ethos across the business. If you can get this right then you have created a powerful voice for your business – the trick then is ensuring that your story, as it evolves, continues to be understood by this army of ambassadors. They are your voice to the customer and beyond. They are your reputation and can damage it with one reckless action.

Keeping them energised and beating a positive rhythm is not easy and will be key to any good long-term marketing communications strategy. This should be approached as you would any external campaign – with the same energy and intelligence. After all, your employees are your greatest asset.

This has become big business for some agencies and also an area of confusion. It is important that your brand lives and breathes in your employees and is conveyed in a way that employees embrace your brand, aspire to work for your brand and feel part of it. This is crucial.

However – over the past decade I have heard of and seen companies where HR departments have created employee brands on their own. A business does not need, nor should it have, multiple brand creators or guardians. This is the beginning of dilution and a weakening of what you stand for.

Don't get me wrong – whilst the core brand should be fairly rigid, its narrative must have some elasticity so it can flex to be relevant for different audiences. Every good marketing communications team will ensure that your brand speaks to your stakeholders such as employees, graduates, prospective new employees, customers, suppliers, investors, governments, politicians, regulators, local communities etc. But that is not a different brand; it is how you nuance your narrative to be relevant.

YOUR EMPLOYEES ARE INDIVIDUALS WALKING TO THEIR OWN RHYTHM

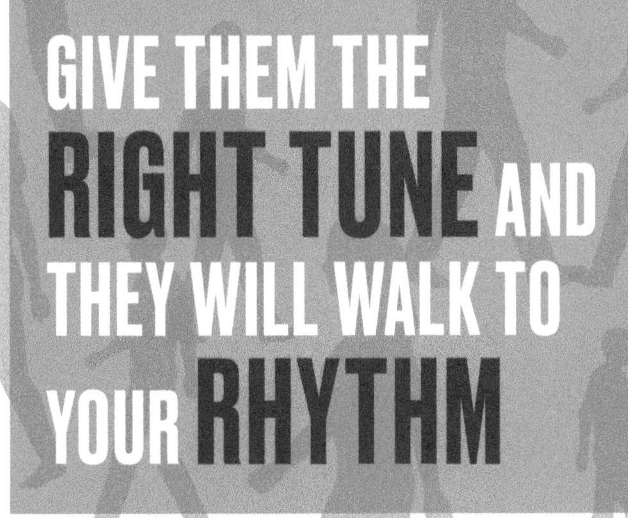
GIVE THEM THE
RIGHT TUNE AND
THEY WILL WALK TO
YOUR RHYTHM

Marketing communications agencies make a significant difference – when leveraged correctly

CREATIVITY, DESIGN, FILM, ADVERTISING, SEO, MEDIA ENGAGEMENT & MONITORING, SOCIAL, TV, NEWS, JOURNALISTS, TRADE, MEASUREMENT

All businesses will need one or more of these skills and experts at some point. Shaping and telling your story, amplifying and getting it out into the world, editing that story for different audiences and creating high-impact messaging is key. There is an army of skills that are required to do this well. It does not need to cost a fortune and certainly cannot be done by one, two or three people. Our digital ecosystems and the global reach that is now possible require specialists. Third-party support also provides a different perspective from your "in-house thinking", and can cross-fertilise ideas from other businesses and sectors. Knowing how to leverage them, and from where, is critical, as they are important if you want to accelerate your ambitions.

Remember – a graphic designer is not just a graphic designer. In this one specialism alone, there are all sorts of different areas of expertise: illustration, infographics, technical drawings, maps, cartoons and so on. You may want all of these at some point, but it is unlikely you will need enough of one to justify keeping someone on the payroll full time. The same goes for many other skills and specialisms that can be found in the world of creative agencies. They are allies who help you amplify your story and become a force multiplier when you need to rapidly expand your intellectual and tactical marketing communications fire-power. The beauty of agencies is that you can ramp up or down your collaborations to suit your budget.

THE PEN IS MIGHTIER THAN THE SWORD

Your story needs to be crafted with the right words and then drawn with the right ink.

POWERFUL MARKETING COMMUNICATIONS IS DELIVERED WHEN YOU LEVERAGE MANY CREATIVE DISCIPLINES THAT CAN MAKE AN IMPACT.

THIS IS WHERE AGENCIES BECOME YOUR BUSINESS'S FORCE MULTIPLIER.

Marketing communications can add $$$ value to your business

TELLING YOUR **STORY**

FLEXING YOUR **MESSAGE**

SHAPING YOUR **NARRATIVE**

DEFINING YOUR **NARRATIVE**

CLARIFYING WHAT YOU **STAND FOR**

MARKETING COMMUNICATIONS DEFINES, OWNS AND MANAGES THE BRAND.

IN TURN, YOUR BRAND HAS A $$$ VALUE.

THEREFORE, A STRONG BRAND CONTRIBUTES TO OVERALL BUSINESS $$$ VALUE.

In the first truth we established that having a story, message and narrative is vital to clarifying who your business is, what you offer, how you do business and how you operate – it's your DNA. It will drive partnerships, trust, sales and who wants to work for you.

Now, how you shape that narrative and your reputation can have a dramatic difference on your $$$ value – brand and business. Simply put – think Microsoft, probably one of the world's most successful B2B organisations. In 2019 its market cap passed the $1 trillion point and by now is over $1.5 trillion. Its brand alone is valued at $326bn.

So, how do you impact that? First a word about your brand – shareholders, investors and customers need to believe in you and your long-term vision and strategy. Clearly a brand like Microsoft is not a pure B2B player and its brand value is boosted by TV advertising, years of being in business and supplying the world's software in our offices and homes. But there is no reason why smaller B2B businesses should not view their brands in similar ways and treat them with a huge amount of respect and sensitivity. Ultimately, the greater care and time taken to nurture your brand, the greater its value will be when one day you have to put a value on it.

Living by your values, embedding your DNA across the organisation, building trust and credibility will all play a part in this value. How you shape your narrative to address specific audiences will be important.

BRAND POSITIONING

For many smaller or mid-sized B2B organisations brand value may only add a small amount to the valuation of the business. This is not to be discounted, of course, but correct positioning of the company could have a more significant impact.

The key is seeing if you can shift the value of your business beyond the sector norm by clearly differentiating your long-term offer from everyone else, which brings us to the benefits of a good narrative (your business and product story) – an important component of the brand.

WHEN IT ALL GOES WRONG

Gerald Ratner managed to wipe $500m off the value of his company when describing his products as crap. A joke, but the joke backfired and within 48 hours his business had lost over $500m in value. Let's just say – your narrative, positive or negative, can impact the business. It's not a joke.

The key is shaping a narrative that demonstrates your long-term journey and ambitions. For game-changing valuations, creating a narrative that completely differentiates your business from everyone else in your sector can dramatically shift the needle.

Even if they are not game-changing, brand valuations and confidence in your business are important and linked to how you tell your story. Investor confusion and misunderstanding of your strategy is such a common issue so make sure that investors are not confused, that they clearly understand your business and, more importantly, treat them like customers – they need to be educated and convinced.

A couple of examples that bring this to life are Ocado and Tesla.

OCADO

FOOD DELIVERY, TECHNOLOGY, PLATFORM INNOVATOR?

Ocado is famous in the UK for transforming the way supermarkets can harness the power of delivery. Known to consumers as a food delivery service, to the business and investment community it is a "centralised distribution" or "warehouse-based" platform. Diversifying its narrative and positioning in two areas demonstrates the innovative nature of the business – important to emphasise. It also positions a growth for the business whose future $ value is hard to ascertain, giving it a $1 billion+ valuation which is not based on today's revenues. It's positioned itself in a space where, owing to the evolving digitisation of retail businesses, investors understand the potential today but it is hard to quantify the value of that potential.

TESLA

CAR MANUFACTURER, TECHNOLOGY / SOFTWARE HOUSE, BATTERY MAKER?

Investors do not necessarily agree on what Tesla is, but one thing is certain – it is not promoting itself as a traditional car manufacturer to the investor community. Big valuations and a 350% stock price rise over 12 months compared to car giant General Motors dropping by 30% in 2020 demonstrate this disparity. Uber is another example of this – is it a taxi company or a tech platform?

BANKRUPTCY AND “CHAPTER 11”

2020 has been the year of businesses going into Chapter 11, entering into special administrative measures etc. The challenge for any business is building trust and credibility in the good times – let alone when you have taken this route and effectively sidelined partners, suppliers and customers. So, rebuilding that trust and credibility is going to be doubly hard. When a business comes out of this, it has to convince the “new investors” that the plan is rock solid, suppliers need to know that you are going to pay and not collapse, and customers and future investors will have to believe in you – all over again. Maybe it is a rebirth but with a lot of naysayers looking on, your narrative and credibility will be key to success.

CHAPTER THREE

4 COMMON MISTAKES

1 STRUCTURE

2 SKILLS

3 REPORTING LINES

4 BUDGET CUTTING

With such a big topic, I have focused on mistakes that can dramatically impact an in-house marketing communications function and its ability to operate effectively or impact an organisation's reputation.

Structure

ONE SHAPE
ONE SIZE
DOES NOT FIT ALL

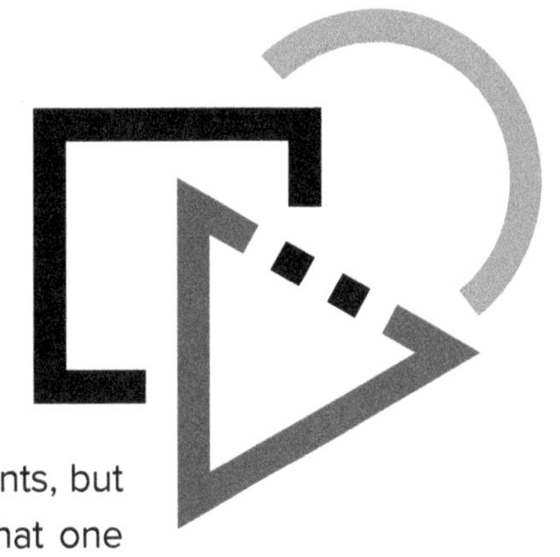

Each business has unique requirements, but more often than not, there is a view that one size (or a few sizes) can fit all. Unfortunately, that is a bit of a cop-out. Shaping your marketing communications unit to match your budgets, strategy, threats and audience needs is really important.

Centralised, devolved and decentralised are common terms for organisational structures, but the reality is the best structure is likely to be a hybrid. Consider where you need to have your strength for the majority of the time. A central engine is great if it can power the marketing communications around the world where you may have small regional or product experts.

However, it is not uncommon for this approach to lead to "structure creep", and suddenly you begin to see roles duplicating in your regions, products or lines of business, which then means rising costs and possible inefficiencies. There is no right or wrong structure, but there is an effective and ineffective use of the skills within that structure.

Regardless of the structure, your brand management and corporate media relations should always be centrally located.

In an ideal world, create a structure that can be flexible and enable you to redirect fire-power from one part of the business to another relatively easily. This can mitigate against downturns in one part of the organisation, enabling you to keep knowledge and talent in the business as opposed to making people redundant.

Skills

Clearly having the right skills is important, but having them in the right place is crucial. A great skill in the wrong place is a waste of money.

As with structures, flexibility is key to both effectiveness and cost. Ensuring that flexibility exists so you can redirect skills quickly and harness their combined power when necessary is the trick. This can benefit the whole organisation as and when it needs to increase or decrease its marketing communications needs.

Establishing the right skills means knowing what your day-to-day requirements are to support sales and manage or grow your reputation combined with being clear on your long-term ambitions. Taking a mid-term view will make a massive difference to the skills you require in-house versus those you can outsource. A good marketing communications strategy aligned to the business objectives will help provide a roadmap for the skills required internally.

Do not be afraid of outsourcing, but do not confuse outsourcing with cost-cutting. Building the right outsourced team requires investment of time and education if you want to get the most out of this approach.

Reporting lines

One of the most common mistakes is to break up marketing communications skills and position them in various silos under different members of the leadership team. This dilutes efficiencies and creates additional barriers to integrated delivery. Also, instead of one function working together for the business, it often results in multiple disciplines competing against each other and fighting for budget.

To avoid this, the most sensible solution is for these skills to be sitting under a leader that understands the marketing communications function and is part of the executive team. Ideally this will be a CMCO, CMO, CDO or similar. Unfortunately, even in this day and age, there are many businesses that still do not have this role or level of role, as its importance remains misunderstood.

Regardless of where you place your team, place it under one leader that will champion its abilities to add value and don't break up the skills and disciplines into various reporting lines. Think about an orchestra – imagine having two or even three conductors. Chaos would ensue and ultimately clashes of rhythm, volume and tempo would occur. It would be less impactful, illogical and expensive.

Budget cutting

I write this with a degree of trepidation as it is such an emotive and complex subject. In B2B organisations, decisions around marketing communications budgets often lack real analysis and can sometimes be emotional reactions. Sometimes it is because the marketing team has never been expected to deliver well-considered budgets aligned to the strategy accompanied by a strong rationale. This has led to a bad rap for the marketing communications professionals that do develop well-considered plans and budgets and has also opened the door for leaders to make cuts that may lack the consideration given to other functions.

Another reason that marketing communications can find itself in a tricky spot is a lack of measurements. This has changed over the past decade and they have come a long way. Another area of contention, but a reality that makes many a CFO nervous, is that there are parts of a marketing budget that will not directly correlate to a “signature on a contract” (especially with long and high-value sales cycles). But, as explained earlier with Newton’s Cradle, just because the team is not there at the contract negotiation, all the “soft” and “hard” tactics deployed to get the sales team to that moment should not be forgotten.

Having said this, regardless of the spend on marketing communications, it is important to know what each element of the budget is doing for the organisation. On too many occasions I have heard of budgets being cut without any analysis of the impact to the organisation – be sure to know what impact any decision will have on sales, reputation, share of voice, events, investor or government relations and so on. If you have a well-planned budget aligned to the business objectives, a cut “should” have an impact on business objectives. An impact analysis will determine the level of risk and whether the cut should be applied.

A final thought on budget cutting. It often seems that a cut of the marketing budget has no apparent immediate impact. However, an empty sales funnel 13–18 months later and no share of voice will set off alarm bells.

MARKETING AND COMMUNICATIONS IS OFTEN THE FIRST LINE OF DEFENCE IN A CRISIS

It is the guardian of the business's reputation and should mobilise rapidly in tough times to protect and defend the business's reputation, credibility and sales messaging. This should combine narrative, PR, advertising and trust-building campaigns.

Despite being so important in times of crisis and even the first line of defence, why is it that the marketing and communications team is often one of the first casualties in cost cutting?

CHAPTER FOUR

3 MYTHS

EVERYONE IS A CREATIVE

MARKETING, BRANDING & SALES ARE THE SAME

B2B OWNERS' PURCHASING IS BASED ON RATIONAL DECISIONS

Everyone is a creative

Contrary to many views, unfortunately a hidden colouring-in talent or sketching ability does not make you an advertiser or marketer. And yet, this simple revelation does not stop many an unqualified individual making highly impactful decisions such as drawing a logo on the back of a piece of paper.

On that basis, anyone that has to balance their household accounts may consider themselves ready to become a CFO.

EVERYONE IS CREATIVE NOT EVERYONE IS A CREATIVE

Marketing, branding & sales are the same

It can be confusing when there is so much overlap, but in reality they have different roles, and whilst I would argue that marketing and branding march together hand in hand, sales is certainly very distinct. One simple way of differentiating: brand is who you are, marketing is how you tell the world who you are and what you are selling, and sales is the outcome. If your branding does not resonate with your audience, regardless of how good your marketing is, things will not move to a sale. Or one dating analogy I liked – if you sound good (marketing) and then look good on the first date (branding), the chances are you will get a second date (sale).

B2B owners, purchasing is based on rational decisions

This is a common misconception that can drive the wrong chain of reactions for your marketing communications decisions and strategy.

If, for example, you believe that business customers are rational and therefore will buy the best product on the market, then an attitude often adopted is “Our product is best so the market will buy it”. That sets off the next reaction in the chain, which will be the marketing messaging which focuses on why you have the best product (technically, speed, size, cost, innovative, heritage etc.) at the expense of what the target customer wants to hear – the reason for purchase.

More importantly, this starting point fails to take into account that most B2B decisions are emotionally driven. A bad decision by a consumer does not lead to losing a job. A bad decision at work can have serious consequences – therefore, ensuring your decision is 100% right is a big driver for a business customer. They will want to hear why a product is going to meet the needs of their business, whether those be savings, sales or efficiencies. It is also worth noting that your message will need to be different for the different internal audiences within a business – the decision-makers and influencers, which will no doubt break down further and all require slightly different messaging.

Remember the phrase from the 80s, "No one got fired for choosing IBM". That is what goes through decision-makers' minds – a roller-coaster of emotions and analysis.

So, taking that into account, if you now start from "What is the customer benefit?" and "Who do I need to convince?", your marketing communications journey will be a little different. That is not to say you do not say why your product is best – it is how you do it, when you do it and who you tell.

NO ONE GOT FIRED FOR CHOOSING IBM

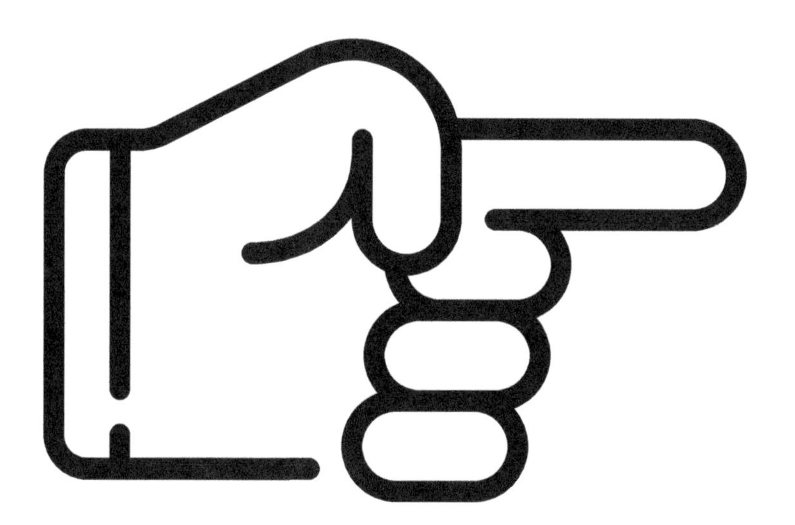

CHAPTER FIVE

2 TIPS

1

SWEAT YOUR BUDGETS

Make sure that wherever possible your marketing investments work hard for you. For example – don't make a CEO video for the annual report. Make a CEO video that can be used in the annual report, company sales kick-off, employee announcement, social media blasts and so on. Think strategically and proactively – not reactively.

2

LET YOUR MARKETING COMMUNICATIONS STRATEGY PLAY OUT

Good results can be achieved quickly, but the best and most enduring impact is achieved when a marketing strategy can evolve and build upon each stage – embedding and driving your message even more deeply each time.

CHAPTER SIX

CONCLUSION

MARKETING COMMUNICATIONS IS NOT A NICE TO HAVE. IT IS A MUST HAVE.

SO...

WHERE DOES THAT LEAVE US?

MARKETING COMMUNICATIONS IS FUNDAMENTAL TO YOUR BUSINESS.

IT SHAPES, BUILDS & PROTECTS YOUR BRAND AND REPUTATION.

IT IS YOUR FIRST LINE OF DEFENCE IN A CRISIS.

IT EDUCATES AND DRIVES THE PASSION OF YOUR NO. 1 ADVOCATES – YOUR EMPLOYEES.

IT IS CRITICAL TO YOUR SALES – KICKING IT OFF, SUPPORTING DURING AND MAINTAINING AFTER.

IT IS MUCH MORE IMPACTFUL WHEN DELIVERED AS AN INTEGRATED FUNCTION.

IT IS NOT ONE PERSON OR ONE SKILL & RELIES ON SKILLS FAR AND WIDE.

IT DOES ADD $$$ VALUE TO YOUR BUSINESS.

SOME SIMPLE STARTING POINTS TO HARNESS THE POWER OF MARKETING COMMUNICATIONS

RECOGNISE WHAT IT CAN DO FOR YOU – BEING CLEAR ON WHAT THE RIGHT MARKETING COMMUNICATIONS STRATEGY CAN ACHIEVE IS KEY. OTHERWISE YOU ARE WASTING YOUR MONEY AND TIME.

FUEL THE PASSION AND CREATIVITY OF YOUR TEAM. DO NOT TREAT THEM LIKE THE AWKWARD TEENAGER THAT COSTS YOU MONEY AND DOES NOT QUITE FIT IN. EMBRACE DIFFERENT THINKING AND RESPECT THEIR KNOWLEDGE.

SET IT UP TO WIN FOR YOU – THE RIGHT STRUCTURE IS THE STARTING POINT.

DON'T CUT BUDGETS WITHOUT KNOWING WHAT WILL BE IMPACTED AND ASK YOURSELF IF RISKING YOUR REPUTATION AND SHARE OF VOICE IS THE RIGHT DECISION.

LEVERAGE EVERY DISCIPLINE AND SKILL TO HARNESS THE POWER AND DELIVER A TRULY INTEGRATED MARKETING COMMUNICATIONS STRATEGY.

CLOSING THOUGHTS

I started writing this book because I wanted to share my passion for delivering good, powerful and effective integrated marketing communications and my belief that, when done well, it can make a significant difference to business outcomes. (Of course, the opposite applies too: when done badly it can be ineffective and wastes valuable budget.)

After more than 20 years of delivering marketing communications solutions to businesses, it had also become clear to me that while many B2B organisations and leaders realised that marketing communications was needed, many did not fully appreciate how and why it was so important. In turn, this meant that marketing functions or disciplines were often undervalued and under-utilised in the areas that really can have an impact.

I hope I have managed to share a few thoughts that you may not have considered – maybe even converted you to championing the power of integrated marketing communications across your business.

If nothing else, hopefully the book will enable richer and better conversations with your marketing communications teams.

ACKNOWLEDGEMENTS

I want to say a big thank you to all my ex team (in-house and agency) who put up with me for a number of years as we shaped and delivered some incredible marketing strategies. It was a fantastic roller-coaster and would not have been nearly as successful, or fun, without you!

A huge thank you to everyone that challenged me during this process, helping me to refine and improve it at each step of the way. Thanks to Richie Parsons who put up with my constant questions on colour printing while focusing on the important task of making the book look great. Also another big thank you goes to my old friend Andrew Currie who has always been there to support, and who kindly read through every draft helping to correct and refine it at each stage.

Finally thanks to my family, and everyone else that supported and encouraged me to get it done and published!

ABOUT THE AUTHOR

Dominic Walters has been working in the world of marketing communications for over 25 years.

Passionate about harnessing the power of integrated marketing communications, Dominic's experience and career have taken him from boutique lobbying agencies through to global multinationals. He has tackled a vast range of marketing communications challenges in most sectors across a diverse range of businesses that have included BP, Shell, PizzaExpress Hong Kong, BAE Systems and Inmarsat Aviation.

His long experience in the industry has led to an in-depth understanding of all aspects of marketing communications.

Lightning Source UK Ltd.
Milton Keynes UK
UKHW021020250121
377617UK00002B/14

9 781838 348809